This title was originally catalogued by the Library of Congress as follows:

599A   Adamson, Joy. Elsa.

Summary: On title page: The true story of a lioness who was brought up from cubhood by Joy Adamson and her husband, a senior game warden; they taught her to stalk and kill for herself so that she could be set free into the African jungle.

"The life story of a lion cub made famous in 'Born Free.' The best photos from the adult book, plus many not included therein, are connected by a very brief and simple running story."—Library Journal.

1. Lions—Pictures, illustrations, etc.   I. Title.

L.C. Catalog Card number: 61-10032   ISBN: 0-394-91117-2 (Lib. ed.)

ELSA

The true story of a lioness who was brought up from cubhood by JOY ADAMSON and her husband, a senior game warden; they taught her to stalk and kill for herself so that she could be set free into the African Jungle

Published by Pantheon Books, New York

© 1961, by Joy Adamson rev. ed 1963
All rights reserved under International and Pan-American Copyright Conventions.
Published in New York by Pantheon Books, a Division of Random House, Inc.
Manufactured in the United States of America

ELSA'S story begins one day when my husband George and I were out with our Land Rover. George had gone off into the bush when he was suddenly charged by a wild lioness. He had to kill her, and it was while he was looking at the beautiful creature that he realized why she had been so angry—she was defending her cubs. He and Nuru, our African boy, searched until they found three tiny lionesses, not more than a few days old, hidden down a hole in a rock. He brought the babies back to me and we took them home. Our rock hyrax, Pati-Pati, who had been with us as a faithful friend for six years, immediately took on the role of nanny and watched over her lively children with great care.

For two days we couldn't persuade them to take any milk at all, but once they found out how delicious canned milk was they could hardly get enough of it.

They were always together and watched anything unusual with great concentration.

We gave them rubber balls and inner tubes to play with. The latter were perfect for games of tug-of-war.

And they were great explorers, setting off in search of adventure all the time. Pati-Pati kept a watchful eye over them.

When they were about ten weeks old and were developing a fancy for books and cushions, we decided to build a door of wire and place it across the entrance to the veranda. The cubs resented this very much, but they soon found plenty to occupy them outside the house—they were particularly fond of playing "King of the Castle" on a potato bag.

Their favorite toy was a sack filled with old rubber tubes which we tied to a branch so that it dangled. They loved hanging on to it, while we pulled and they swung high in the air.

One day when they were nearly four months old and I was out for a walk with them they met our donkeys. The little cubs with all the courage of grown lions immediately stalked and charged them. They were so pleased with their success that a few days later they put to flight all forty of our pack donkeys and mules.

They were also great climbers and liked to get high up in the branches of trees.

When the cubs were about five months old we realized that we couldn't possibly keep three fast-growing lions in the house, so we regretfully decided that the two bigger ones should be sent to the Rotterdam Zoo and that we would keep Elsa, who was the smallest and who had the most engaging character. Opposite is a picture of her.

Elsa was very upset at the loss of her sisters as she now had to play by herself or with the boys. We decided to take her with us on a trip which, as it happened, George had to make at that time. Luckily, she loved the outdoor life as much as we did, and she used to go off on little explorations of her own. We also started to teach her to retrieve, and she soon knew that "bang" meant dead bird.

Her food now consisted mainly of raw meat, mostly sheep and goat. She liked to lick out the marrow from the bones while I held them for her. Sometimes I had to scratch it out, and then she licked it off my fingers—her tongue was exceedingly rough. After she had had her supper she often dozed off with my thumb still in her mouth.

Elsa now began to meet other wild animals. She was quite fearless and would chase a whole herd of elephants. She particularly enjoyed stalking giraffe, who did not seem to mind but just watched while she wriggled toward them on her tummy. One day when she thought we had spoiled her stalk by standing up and watching her she got very cross, rushed back, and knocked us to the ground!

When Elsa was about a year old our leave fell due and we decided to spend it on the shores of the Indian Ocean. The journey took us three days, and to my great distress Pati-Pati, who had been such a faithful friend to me for seven and a half years, died of a heat stroke shortly after we had set off. As soon as we arrived we all went down to the beach to introduce Elsa to the sea. To our surprise she loved it.

She enjoyed, among many other games, trying to catch a coconut which George used to swing on a string.

Soon after our return George had to make another trip, this time to Lake Rudolf. It was a long weary journey of three hundred miles and Elsa travelled in the back of my truck. As soon as we arrived at the lake she rushed into the water to cool and clean herself from the heat and dust of travelling. She did not worry one bit about the crocodiles which swim about there in great numbers.

We had sent the pack donkeys on ahead, and when we arrived they were very anxious to be rid of their loads. Elsa had to be firmly held back from attacking or chasing them.

We walked for about seven or eight hours each day, Elsa often dipping herself in the lake to keep cool. She preferred walking early in the morning or late in the evening; and through the heat of the day, especially during our afternoon break, she liked to share my camp bed for a short nap.

On our return home Elsa began to show an increasing interest in going off on her own. She was nearly two years old and her voice was getting much deeper. Often she stayed away for two or three days and we knew that she several times joined up with other lions. But she was as affectionate as ever when she saw us again.

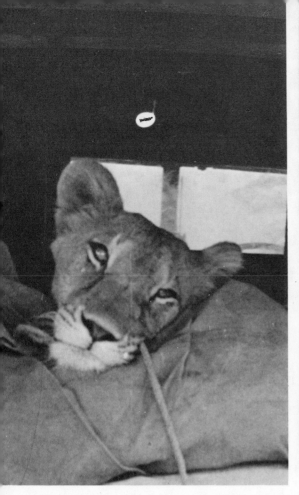

We now began to wonder whether we could release Elsa back to the wild instead of sending her to join her sisters, as we had originally intended. It would be an experiment worth trying, and we thought we would take her to a place where there was plenty of game, spend two or three weeks with her, and if all went well leave her.

Elsa travelled in the back of my truck and the morning after our arrival we took off her collar to show her that she was free. She hopped onto the roof of the Land Rover and we set off to explore the territory.

We introduced her to a very handsome young lion whom we met, but although he seemed very friendly she was suddenly overcome by shyness. We left her with him one night, but the next morning when we went back he had disappeared and Elsa was alone, frantically pleased to see us.

Up to now we had always given her her meat cut up. Although she knew how to retrieve we were not sure whether she knew how to cope with a dead animal, but if she was to be left alone she would have to learn. To our surprise and delight we discovered that even though she had had no mother to teach her she knew exactly what part of an animal was eatable and what should be buried. But she had no idea how to kill. However, we left her where there was plenty of game, hoping that hunger would force her to attack.

But she hated being left on her own and when we went to see her she was terribly hungry and had obviously not eaten since our last visit. After we had given her a meal she fell sound asleep.

Quite obviously we could not leave her yet, so we applied for permission to take our overseas leave in Africa. This was granted. But shortly after this Elsa became very ill and her whole education was interrupted. When she recovered we decided to move her to a climate which would suit her better. The new home we chose for her was only some twenty miles from her birthplace. It was a really beautiful place with a river running through it where many wild animals came to drink.

Most of the tree trunks had been rubbed smooth by elephants, and Elsa found it difficult to do her daily claw exercises. Only the baobabs were untouched, and Elsa found those with hollow trunks particularly attractive.

I decided to make a studio beside the river under the shade of an overhanging tree. Elsa was a little suspicious of the typewriter at first, but she soon grew used to it and liked to lie at my feet while I wrote her story.

Every morning we took Elsa for a walk so that she would get used to the surrounding countryside.

If we were only going a short distance she liked to ride on the roof of the Land Rover.

We stayed with her for several months while she learned all the things her own mother would have taught her. As part of her training we killed a buffalo, and after we had dragged the heavy beast back to the camp she spent the whole night guarding it. At first we did most of the killing, but she always helped us and soon learned to kill on her own.

From then on, we watched for an opportunity to leave her. One afternoon she refused to go for a walk with us and disappeared until the next morning. We realized she had made friends with a wild lion and that the time had now come.

We therefore drove to another river ten miles away where we planned to spend a week before returning to see how she had managed without us. Although I knew it was for her good, I could not help feeling we were deserting her.

At last the week of waiting ended. On our return we fired a shot and Elsa came rushing out of the bush, overjoyed to see us. She was thin but not hungry, for she showed no interest in the buck we had brought her.

A few days later when we were out for a walk Elsa disappeared toward the river. Soon we heard some extraordinary noises and went to investigate. Elsa was sitting on a buffalo in the middle of the river: she must have leaped at it as it was crossing and when it slipped pressed home her attack. George immediately put the buffalo out of its misery with a bullet.

We now had the problem of getting the buffalo out of the water. At first Elsa tried to do this alone and did not want us to help. But suddenly to our amazement she realized we would all have to work together; and with the boys helping she got the beast onto the bank.

After this we paid her short visits at frequent intervals, and although she was always delighted to see us it was quite obvious that she could manage without us. I went to England for a long time that summer, and after my return she was particularly pleased to see me.

We had always hoped that she would find a mate and that one day she would walk into our camp followed by a family.

You can imagine our great joy when a few months later she swam across the river followed by three fine cubs.

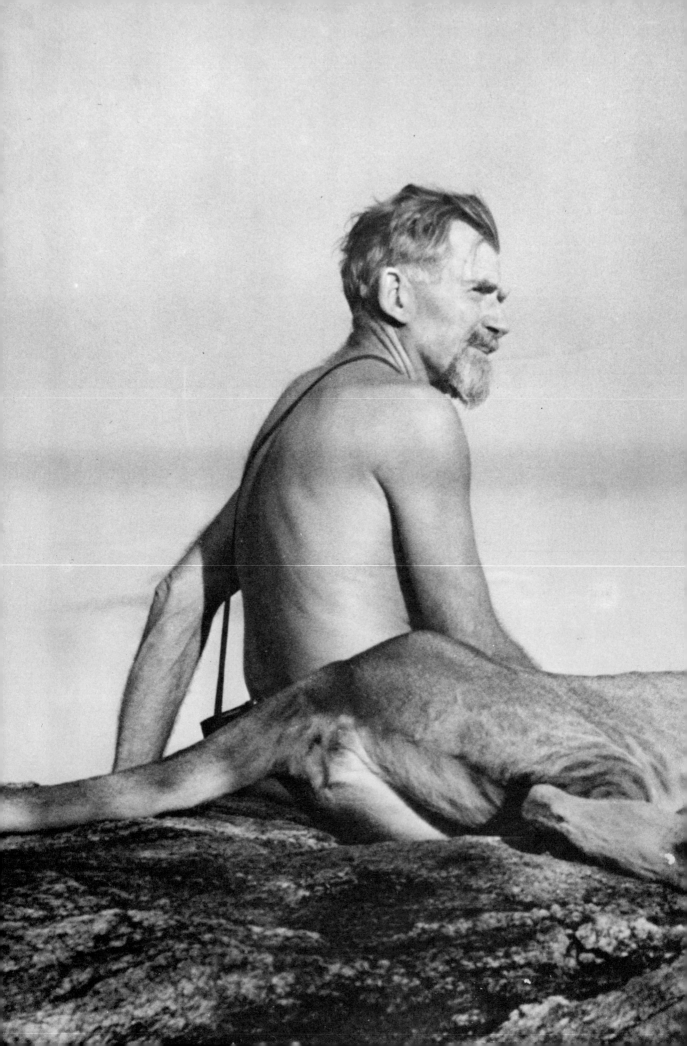